BOAT

MISS AVALON

BY ALEX SUMMERS

Rourke
Educational Media
rourkeeducationalmedia.com

Scan for Related Titles
and Teacher Resources

Teaching Focus:

Concepts of Print: Have students find capital letters and punctuation in a sentence. Ask students to explain the purpose for using them in a sentence.

Before Reading:

Building Academic Vocabulary and Background Knowledge

Before reading a book, it is important to set the stage for your child or student by using pre-reading strategies. This will help them develop their vocabulary, increase their reading comprehension, and make connections across the curriculum.

1. Read the title and look at the cover. *Let's make predictions about what this book will be about.*
2. Take a picture walk by talking about the pictures/photographs in the book. Implant the vocabulary as you take the picture walk. Be sure to talk about the text features such as headings, the Table of Contents, glossary, bolded words, captions, charts/diagrams, or Index.
3. Have students read the first page of text with you then have students read the remaining text.
4. Strategy Talk – use to assist students while reading.
   - Get your mouth ready
   - Look at the picture
   - Think…does it make sense
   - Think…does it look right
   - Think…does it sound right
   - Chunk it – by looking for a part you know
5. Read it again.

Content Area Vocabulary
Use glossary words in a sentence.

anchor
drives
engine
stern

After Reading:

Comprehension and Extension Activity

After reading the book, work on the following questions with your child or students in order to check their level of reading comprehension and content mastery.

1. *Where is the engine on a boat? (Summarize)*
2. *What do you call the person who drives a boat? (Asking Questions)*
3. *Where can you see boats in your city or town? (Text to self connection)*
4. *What are the front and the back of the boat called? (Asking Questions)*

Extension Activity

Make Your Own Wax Boat! Have a parent or adult buy some wax at a craft store. Or you can use the wax coating that comes on cheese from the grocery store. Mold the wax by rolling it in your hands to make it soft and easier to shape your boat. Now, create your own boat shape. You can even cut out a triangle out of a piece of paper and stick a toothpick through the top and bottom and attach it to the wax. Fill a small pool or bowl with water and float your boat!

Table of Contents

Boat Ride!

Ready to go!

How will I get there?

I know! I will take a boat. The captain helps me onboard.

I put on my life vest.
The captain **drives**
the boat.

Parts of a Boat

The **engine** is in the back. It powers the boat to move.

engine

The bottom of the boat is called the hull. The front of the boat is called the bow.

bow

The back of the boat is called the **stern**.

stern

It speeds across the water. The wind blows my hair.

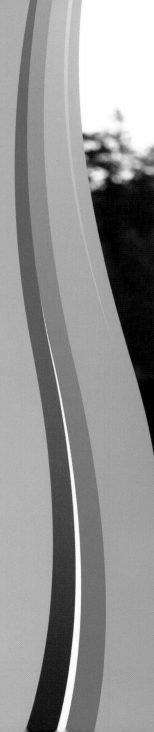

The boat slows down.
The captain turns the
engine off.

Anchor Down!

He puts down the **anchor**. It keeps the boat from floating away.

anchor

I throw in my pole. I am ready to go fishing!

Picture Glossary

 **anchor** (ANG-kur): A metal object that is lowered from a boat when it stops to keep it from drifting.

 **drives** (DRIVES): When you drive, you are taking someone somewhere in a vehicle, like a boat.

 **engine** (EN-jin): A machine that makes something move by using energy.

 **stern** (sturn): The rear end of a ship or boat.

Index

Websites to Visit

www.boatsafe.com/kids/index.htm

www.discoverboating.com/beginner/safety/boating-with-kids.aspx

www.boatingorders.com/books.html

About the Author

Alex Summers enjoys all forms of transportation. Especially if they are taking her to places she has never been or seen before. She loves to travel, read, write, and dream about all the places she will visit someday!

Meet The Author!
www.meetREMauthors.com

Library of Congress PCN Data

Boat / Alex Summers
(Transportation and Me!)
ISBN 978-1-68342-164-1 (hard cover)
ISBN 978-1-68342-206-8 (soft cover)
ISBN 978-1-68342-233-4 (e-Book)
Library of Congress Control Number: 2016956536

Rourke Educational Media
Printed in the United States of America,
North Mankato, Minnesota

www.rourkeeducationalmedia.com

Edited by: Keli Sipperley
Cover design by: Tara Raymo
Interior design by: Rhea Magaro-Wallace
Photo Credits: Cover © Annese, enjoying, zagar; Title page © Aneese; page 5 © shapecharge, ez_thug, JackF, Nerthuz, terasov_vl; page 7, 17, 19 © Albert Pego; page 9 © FlairImages; Page 11 © TakePhoto; page 13 © rmanera; page 15 © LUNAMARINA; page 21 © eAlisa; page 22 © holbox

Also Available as: